To the wild devas of nature

Dedicated to the teacher, lover, healer, and warrior
within each of us in this time of change

DANCE THROUGH IT

CAMI RENFROW

"And I will show that nothing can happen more beautiful than death."
Walt Whitman

"If your knees have not buckled in ecstasy while standing when a veil parts. If a cherished tear of gratitude has not sung leaping from your eye. If anything your palm does touch cannot help reveal the Beloved. My words are full of golden secrets that are not too hard to crack, and will remedy one hundred fears and ills." Hafiz

I'm going to tell you a true story, the best I can. It's a story that came about in a strange way: a hardy seed of unknown origin pressed into weedy, fertile soil. At first I couldn't penetrate the gift I had been given, couldn't see what it was all about and certainly couldn't find any way to harvest it. But over time it germinated and sprouted, put down roots and grew into a luscious tree with distinct branches and leaves and fruits. Now there's plenty to share.

CATALYST

When I was 22 I was in a car accident on my way to work one wet morning. Speed and carelessness, high winds and rain-soaked roads: it was really not the safest time to sing along raucously with Alanis Morissette. I lost control, a gust of wind caught me, and I swerved head-on into a mountainside at 70 miles an hour.

Flipping end over end up the slope, my rag doll body launched through the windshield onto the muddy mountainside. The rain-softened slope of the earth absorbed my body's impact with a spongy hug. The car continued upward until gravity took over, and it bounced back down the mountain.... to fall on me. I was crushed belly down with a red hatchback waving its little broken bug legs in the air. It pinned my face sideways, neck twisted, arms and legs jumbled, my entire broken body compressed by the car above. Passersby arrived before the tires had stopped spinning.

The first person to stop searched all around the scene for the driver who must have been thrown free. Then he saw the strands of long blond hair sticking out under the crumpled car. Expecting no sign of life, he reached down to squeeze the only thing he could reach - my fingertips.

The moment of transition from this life is undertaken alone, for each of us. But as my body launched through the windshield, it pitched me headlong through the limits I had known in life as a human being, and I emerged into the deep familiarity and recognition of the Tribe of Life itself. Peace permeated my awareness, and a love that for years brought a cry of gratitude just from the memory. A primal space within recognized this state of being from before birth, from between lives. (Lives! There were so many of them!) I felt the bright embrace of being recognized, truly known and understood, and fully, actively loved in spite of it all by the flavors and whispers of life present. I was clean, and I was home. Time and space fell away as the constructs they are, and I expanded into a sense of connection and simultaneous awareness of the inner intentions of every energetic body there. Although these energies could be distinct, the overriding truth was clear: together we were one intertwined, infinite Being, connected through full innate awareness and sentience of all life at once. So dazzling and convincing was it all that my current life and identity dropped away unnoticed like clothes carelessly shed onto the floor.

It seemed the whole of existence and human experience permeated the air, retrievable with the flick of intention: every language, every tear drop, every shed skin cell, every body of music, every story, every loss, every secret. It was everything I'd ever wanted to learn, everything there was to learn, right there ready to spring into awareness with the slightest intention. More vivid and self-evident than anything I had experienced in life as a human, it still is the most undeniable thing I've ever witnessed. I'd trust the knowing that came from this, before answering the simplest fact like "What's your name?" or "When were you born?". As much as those things seem like they have a straightforward answer, this deep level of knowing made them look like fun trivia you'd memorize about a character in a book. So this was death. Now I remembered.

I basked in this warm love, then recognized a reunion with the energies of people I loved. I could sense the family back on earth present when I searched for them, as if right there inside me. We were more closely connected than we had ever been in life, with no bodies or sense of separation to get in our way. A jumble of energies of my soul group, my teammates in evolution, people who had already died or who were waiting out this incarnation, greeted me in an embracing homecoming. It was every love I've ever heard whispered in my heart, all present at once. I felt an intertwined connection to each person or being or place that ever meant anything in the previous life, only it was so much more enduring and deliberate than the mere earthly bonds we had shared no matter how important those bonds seemed at the time. People who had been gone from my life were not really gone.

We go on. And on and on. Whether in a linear fashion – life after life - or in a broader sense, of interweaving with everyone who ever was, reincarnation was self-evident as soon as the veil was dropped. I had had many lives – could vaguely see them over there on the left, long-discarded clothes hanging in a closet (personality, physical characteristics, quirks, loves, challenges, griefs, irritating habits, the unique combination of sunlight and sulphur and sea salt that made up that particular body). More lives were coming, and this was the recharging space for reviewing and choosing anew.

I was shown a 'bank' of recently dead people (who were no longer people of course, and couldn't even be seen – they were just energetic entities I could sense – and in fact seemed to be part of me – part of this Force of Love - as much as they were separate beings). Many had died tragic, unexpected deaths. All were full of joy. Of all the beautiful agony we could see in the loved ones remaining on earth, all of it appeared noble. All of it appeared purposeful. These recently dead were trying to comfort and communicate with the earthly human part of those left behind, nearly laughing with compassionate outreach. It was as if they were trying to wrap their arms around their loved ones and say, "Can't you feel me? I'm right here with you even more than in life because my half of the veil is lifted. No body or personality holds me back from you. I did my job, I died when I was supposed to. Your job is beginning. We are a team, we chose this together, it's your turn to grow from this and transform it with your open heart. After this life we'll plan another together as we have so many times. In the meantime let's get this one right and make good use of your pain for the benefit of all of life. Everything is exactly as it should be and I wouldn't change it if I could. The only shame of this whole mess is if you let it destroy you and waste the chance for growth. Are you sure you can't feel me?" It was almost a sense of coaching and cheering and reassuring.

This sense was so powerful that for years after I returned to a more normal type of consciousness, anytime I heard of a tragedy too big to recover from (losing three children in one day for example) my instinctive first emotion was a genuine sense of gaping awe and respect for the people involved, admiration that they would sign on for such difficulties, and for the potential for growth and useful power in proportion to their pain.

In addition, some of this communication seemed to go on between recently dead and people back in the world who were NOT loved in this life but perhaps nemeses(!). They were part of the soul group and beloved teammates in growth nonetheless, and the sense of love between them at that higher level was equal to that between people who had played a pleasant role in each other's lives.

A loving, personal presence helped me realize it was time to review the recently discarded life. I had been so busy wondering and gawking that it was with a jolt I remembered the crumpled clothes left there on the floor – my life, identity, relationships, memories. As recognition kicked in about which one it was, I felt a compassionate and distant fondness for it. Life after 'death' was so much larger, so much more brilliant, that the earthly life left behind no longer seemed very important. But each life is crucial, because that's how we learn. So I picked it up, dusted it off, and hung it up for review.

(This was the only part of the experience that had a sense of time – a realization that it was now time for a transition. Otherwise time seemed to be only an occasionally useful construct rather than part of the fabric of reality. To break the flashes into stages I have to narrate its shape with space and time, because that's the way we conceive our world. But it didn't happen in any special order or place. Heaven isn't 'up there'. It isn't even a place. Even when we leave our bodies we aren't really even going 'up there' except in the more material, earthly perception. There is no 'up there'. There is no first this, then this, then finally that. Cause and effect, the path taken and the path untaken, the before and after, fate and free will, inside and outside, me over here and you over there... they are all illusions of the one piece of fabric that weaves it all together. Time and space are necessary constructs to tell the story.)

From the field of unwavering love came an abstract chorus of loving support and understanding gathered to review with me. At the same time, non-duality was so pervasive that we all seemed to be the same being, feeling each other's truth and presence fully – I was them, together we were God, the Tao, life itself. There was no Other. This council wasn't there to judge me. It was there to lend compassionate support as I witnessed the Mirror, now from the benefit of a transcendent perspective. My role on earth to that point was over, the lessons ready to be digested.

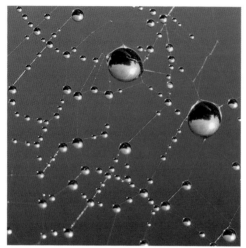

Photo by Luc Viatour

Here I could see the whole picture, how every thought and motivation of the previous life passage snaked tendrils of manifestation into the world and how each tendril rolled out to affect other people and all of life. I felt everything. Every little kindness. Every subtle dig, each moment of carelessness, the wasted potentials, the comfort passed on to others, the secret joys, impatience, self-pity, a genuine smile to a lonely person at the right moment.... Ripples from a tossed pebble, I experienced how everyone experienced my actions and intentions, and how everyone they affected felt, and so on down the chain of action and reaction flowing even into nature itself. More importantly, I could see the bar – how things could have been if enacted with pure love. Each action was balanced by its effect on the life force in total. The chain ran from my link back up, retracing and revealing why I made the choices I did, why my full intentions were not in alignment with my professed goals, saw the causes and effects throughout multiple lifetimes. It was as if the web of this incarnation was a soft silk and we were holding it up to examine thread by thread, seeing how it draped in all directions from each point we lifted, seeing where the tensions ran through other layers and other lifetimes. With this review there was no blame, no shaming, no rejection. The supportive sense around me remained lovingly, fully understanding, as if actively trying to both celebrate the successes and compassionately witness the total alongside me.

Regardless of who we are, we're ALL embraced with loving compassion at death and throughout our lives. We are never out of the light, not any part of us. I saw that imagining ourselves to have parts that are hidden from the light is its own punishment, but the light is always there, patiently and fully shining on anything we're willing to expose. We are our own judge, and the dark of our separation must be its own hell in the end. The review was overwhelmingly a time of gratitude, ecstasy, joy and surprise from the chain of good effects from small loving actions. I saw how easily our most subtle intentions ripple through the life surrounding us, and how kind acts must be accompanied by self-honesty to have their full power, how good acts lose their power if they are accompanied by misaligned intentions. I could see that the same joy of heaven on earth can be created as a living force while we're alive.

I pretty much scrapped any remaining guilt about culturally-derived morals after this process and rebuilt mine from the ground up. Love is the only thing that matters, the highest and most transcendent love possible. Of course in this earthly world trying to operate from this deeper love has to involve frank self-honesty about intentions and the visceral recognition that anything we do to others we do directly to ourselves. Don't think of passive love and light. This deep love is active, and it has to apply to one's self as much as to others – love may call for anger over injustice, enforcing boundaries, and holding one's own needs as valid.

Here, in reviewing the past, we planned the future. As part of the life review I willingly laid out the challenges and flaws of the next stage of incarnation (which ended up being in the same life and body). Like all spirits in the review process, this benevolent team of energies and I chose together to leverage past strengths for the good of others and for future growth, to put certain obstacles in place for the better flow of the stream. I worked out with my soul group what roles we were to play in the coming life this time, cruel antagonists appreciated equally to tender lovers. This was co-choreography of the life ahead, a complex dance planned with a bit of room for improvisation. Although we were aware of the difficulties we were taking on and certainly didn't desire them for the sake of suffering, we yearned for the growth and ultimate reunion the lessons would bring us. No one I saw was eager to again experience the separation brought by the veil of illusion – the veil that makes us believe we are all distinct, finite beings, the veil that offers us the narrative of time and space.

Despite the reluctance to slip again into the confusion of duality, separation and polarity, I felt a sense of resolve, determination and honor and an eagerness to enact my mission. (Oh, but to figure out what the mission is once back in duality! That's another book!) Cheering well-wishes rose from behind the curtain as I headed out to take the stage.

Unconscious from the moment the car landed on my back, every inch pinned to the earth, I felt a big, warm hand squeeze my fingers. Concern passed directly from his skin into mine. My first conscious thought was scrambling to make sense of the compressed and dark space I found myself in, with a calm third-party detachment. The first words to form in my head were "Oh – this must be the car accident she was about to have" while not quite yet remembering who 'she' was. Face sticky with blood and mud, from one eye I could barely spy the hint of shadows of people darting around trying to help as I heard the man brokenly yelling "She's alive!"

I felt a distinct, instantaneous scan of my whole body and psyche, as if I was being zipped back together. Everything was accounted for and everything matched. I witnessed that I would be fine, that this attempt at continuing in the same body had a chance. I felt a bit of surprise that the body and soul should pair back up properly, already so changed from their previous fit.

"I cannot be awake for nothing looks to me as it did before, Or else I am awake for the first time, and all before has been a mean sleep."
Walt Whitman

I had a sense of having been long ago and far away and returning with a new level of awareness available, a sense of an older and wiser part of me that had been awakened. It transcended fear. This familiar, august higher presence gave me an innate sense of acceptance and awareness that this was a great honor and opportunity, and in some hidden core I felt a thirst to undergo it. This peace and purpose is not something I had to talk myself into at a conscious level – it was self-evident, and a tremendous comfort. But I had no memory of where I had been, and the present moment was much too busy to stop and figure it out. It was almost like having leaped into a character and scrambling to understand who you're playing and what they're supposed to do next.

Higher self-presence notwithstanding, I was being crushed to death. Third-party calm could only last so long. My heart couldn't beat and I struggled to inflate my lungs against the weight. The instinct for survival kicked in with a healthy panic to escape the immediate suffering, although there was no fear of death itself. The frame of my perspective immediately reduced to the very, very human experience of feeling life compressed slowly out of me, of my pulses and rhythms bowing to the beast on my back. I begged the shadows above for a gasping help: "I can't breathe! I can't breathe!"

I could hear my rescuers hurriedly organizing themselves to lift the car off and let it roll downhill, and then my awareness split into three perspectives: From below, I watched as they lifted the car off me, four bodies stretched out tall with the sun shining through between them from the sky above. From above, I watched as they lifted the car off me, four bodies stretched out tall with light shining up between them from underneath the car. And from my belly-down position I saw nothing but blood and darkness and fuzzy shadows in the farthest corner of sight, but felt and heard them lift the car off me with my face turned away downhill.

Which of these is the truth? It took me a whole year to see the inconsistency here, because our brains are wonderful at explaining away the unexplainable. It wasn't until describing this moment to someone out loud that I finally recognized an awareness of at least three views at once. With this particular witnessing, there was no sense of mysticism, no sense of light or peace or greater expansion. It was a mundane out of body experience and took me a year to notice the matter-of-fact conflict of facts: that I had experienced three perspectives at once.

(Here I'll mention what a friend said the first time I told him about this. He earnestly wondered, "How do you know it wasn't all in your head?" The question made me laugh out loud because – How else could it be? It certainly wasn't something that happened in my body! No one saw me hovering up there, a body double. 'In our head' is perspective, isn't it? And besides, there's really no head and no inside so no head to be inside. More on the inadequacies of words, coming up.)

Several confusing minutes later the EMTs arrived and I was loaded by stretcher into an ambulance. There was a brief flash – like a subliminal frame in a filmstrip – and I looked down from above again, this time on a bloodied head and face with big white eyes peeking out from the thick sticky red. It could have been anyone under there. I didn't feel scared, but those eyes sure looked it. The EMTs asked if I was having trouble breathing, and back in the body again I remember trying to speak as truthfully as possible when answering "Only when I was under the car", prompting their amused laughs.

BEYOND OUR SKIN

Shock is a process of astonishing self-preservation, allowing us to get from an emergency to help before crumbling. Help had come to me, but the girl who shuffled herself sideways onto a stretcher that morning was in a hospital bed unable to move her legs by nighttime.

The seat of our whole being – the pelvis and sacrum that we sit on and lay on and walk with – had cracked into countless fractures. The base of the spine had split in two, both shoulders were spit out of their sockets, a hairline skull fracture left blood dripping out of my ears, and blood clots and a brand new ringing clogged my hearing. The force of impact burst splits into my skin like a squashed grape along either side of the ribcage and hips. Doctors used words like shattered, and exploded. Medical testing was so focused on the potentially life threatening issues, that less important broken bones went unnoticed by all of us until after they were further healed. There was too much noise in the body for me to possibly hear them.

I was lost in a black flame, unable to distinguish any part of the dark from another, unable to even find the boundaries of my own body, unable to understand anything happening inside of me because every sensation had been scrambled. And what a silly thing the word 'pain' is! A word – especially an insubstantial single syllable like that - can't come close to the self-immolating ink that dissolved every part of the young woman lying in that bed. Because so much of the core of the body had been damaged, there seemed to be no steady center where thoughts and emotions could come to rest. Pain swallowed my concept of myself and my boundaries and later reduced my actions and plans to one painstaking, costly motion at a time, moment after moment, week after week.

This was my first recognition that we usually witness the world from a certain space within us. Where is your awareness centered right now? Often it's right from the center of the head, sometimes it's coming out the brow, sometimes we're resting peacefully in the hara – the belly. With the core of the body inaccessible, my witness sense was searching desperately for a place to settle. The Chinese have a term for this: shen deficiency, when awareness flutters around looking for a nest like a bird unable to land.

For days I lay in the same position on my back in that hospital bed, listening to the soft pump of the air mattress as it filled and drained its pockets, filled and drained, passively shifting the weight of my body's broken pressure points because I couldn't do it myself. After a couple of days of being lost inside the black flame cloud, it mercifully shifted. I was no longer inside of it, and could begin to modify and shape it, to interact with it – to play with it - to see myself as a separate being from the pain and even begin to sense where it was localized. It no longer engulfed me. This was my first conscious exposure to noticing, conceptualizing, and manipulating the pranic and etheric energies that make up our bodies. It was the first wave of the fierce inner training in energetic healing I was about to undergo. I found I could influence my experience of pain – however pitifully – by pushing and tugging on these thick windy snarled tendrils of dense presence. Something deep in my heart, my throat, my gut and palms and forehead reached out through my skin to interact with this heavy body now present in my awareness. And there was something else strange. While some parts of me were working as normal (like hands and forearms) I understandably couldn't initiate movements that came from the trunk, like rotate my toes, or use my limp shoulders, or shift my rump a millimeter. But was it really Couldn't? Wasn't it more like Wouldn't try? It seemed that my Will would not even send the impulse along the traumatized nerves to the muscles to act. Something deeper than the muscles was injured, or resting. Something that refused to act. The tiniest movements – or impulses to move - became fascinating as I noticed subtleties that had all happened automatically before.

Between bursts of lucid conversation and interaction with loved ones and hospital staff, life was reduced for hours to the space between inhale and exhale, exhale and inhale. Time ticked on, breath after breath, and my sole earthly task was to force that unwilling ribcage and groaning spine to take in air and – unrelentingly - return to task later to push it out. In between those exhales and inhales, though.... a world was opening up.

Struggle to inhale.... blissful release... brace for the exhale.... merciful release..... force the inhale... I drifted further and further between breaths. My physical boundaries suddenly melted and I felt a sense of release from the body. I found myself taking up the space of the whole room, taking up the space of the whole town, expanding anywhere and nowhere. A sense of deep, profound familiarity and recognition settled in as I woke up from the dream of having been a body-bound person, and rejoined – for the first time since birth - a reality of far more clarity and depth than anything I've witnessed in even the most vivid worldly experiences. Between breaths, I simply slipped from one form of consciousness into a much more spacious and connected and powerful one.

From this state I felt honored to keep the body breathing and endure this particular blazing burden. It wasn't suffering, it was fuel. I was filled with the sheer joy and gratitude of experiencing this particular delicious incarnation, this body and personality. This joy of Self has returned over and over through the years, at times gracing me with a sense of being blessed at every pleasure and pain of being in the flesh. I believe now that this space of being is our birthright and available in any life, once we let go of our definitions and expectations about what we are. In hospice volunteer situations I've seen people in what I believe to be this state in their final days and months, talking with long-gone friends and startled by unexpected visions and messages, as the veil slowly becomes more permeable. It is a gift to us. I don't believe life and death are binary states.

Although my body was reduced to a crumpled mess, I felt more powerful than ever before in life, as though I was churning through greater work – more important work - during that time in bed than I had ever accomplished with a healthy mind and body. It felt as if every minute of enduring purchased something for life itself. Each of my senses and organs, my nervous system: my body seemed to be remodeling itself, burning with light and transformation. This feeling was to return later – fierce and prolonged - in the years to come. Even in vital health, the body seems to be but a small part of the whole human - a crystallized formation of the greater being. I felt infinite, purposeful, powerful, ecstatic, connected, and necessary. Every hair and pore felt sacred, the body as gateway to spirit with beauty and light glowing from between each cell.

I believe it is in this state of being that we find the ability to seep into another's experience (or into communion with nature) by going beyond what we consider "us" in a material sense. The ability to receive insight that's personally potent comes from this state, whether we interpret it as coming from others or coming from within our own boundaries.

Seeping back and forth from the world between breaths, I was unable to speak, and unwilling to tarnish the holiness with words. Only the concepts 'One' and 'All' would come at first. At one point I returned to the body for a breath feeling 'I AM' blazed across my forehead, filling my chest with its inarguability. I think it was my spirit's last ditch attempt to get a message across the void and make it into my struggling conscious mind.

That particular corner of the white hospital ceiling was becoming a fast friend. (Days later, when I was moved for the first time, I remember how very refreshing and stimulating it felt to look up at it from a new angle.) Flowers cheered the room, more every day, until they peeked from every surface. Volunteers came in one morning to wash the dark purple snarl my hair had become, as everyone wondered if it would just need to be shaved off. Those loving ladies scrubbed my hair inch by inch, refilling the water basin over and over until the water ran clear. Then shifts of friends and family painstakingly combed each inch through six hours and two bottles of detangler, soaking love into every brushstroke, until they finally accomplished a tender kindness: my hair flowed long and soft again.

Most days were much quieter. Creaky inhale... drift away.... snagged exhale... return... open those ribs inhale.... I drifted deeper yet. Then the world ended as if someone had spun the telescope focus.

Photo by John Charlton

I crossed into a state that was deep, fundamental, irreducible. An ocean of exquisite sensitivity, of omnisentience (sensing everywhere at once), turned me inside out to reveal itself at the core. Losing every sense of distinction, I floated as part of this gloriously intelligent web of light. Even the awesome flavors and energies from previous states of consciousness looked trivial compared to this luminous irreducible force, this field of existence. It seemed to be an order of magnitude different from the earlier experiences. This was the force of consciousness itself. There was no 'I' left whatsoever, not even the broad perspective from the life review. My boundaries as a human and as a spirit were completely erased. Witnessing from a localized single point, my perspective was simultaneously spread through the multidimensional, non-localized perspective of the entire web. There was no end and no beginning, like the lake underneath the forms that dance through our lives.

This was beyond bliss, beyond truth, beyond peace and ecstasy and all the searing emotions of the previous stages. It was stillness in the middle, consciousness without form.

In the distance a gentle wave swelled up, moving across the ocean of light toward the point of perspective assigned to me. As it arose I became aware that this wave was the concerns, prayer, and emotions being streamed toward me from hundreds of people I knew in this life and from many others who had only heard about my situation. My point of perspective rose as the wave reached it, and correspondingly I was lifted, just a little, from the pain in my body. It became a little lighter to bear.

I had just viscerally witnessed prayers and intentions became physical, tangible reality. (In using the word 'prayer' I mean something an atheist could easily do as well as a theologian – no special form, just focused will propelled by the power of love and concern.) It was made known to me that this was Consciousness creating Form through Intention. Nothing exists until it rises into form on this field. Every single bit of material in the world – even the computer or paper you're reading this on, and the stardust that nourishes your marrow, and the paint on the wall, and the dog you love, and each single hair on his loppy ear – must have begun there on the sacred field of consciousness, shaped by the impulse of intention. There is no 'there' there.

Coming back into this human life, this is the single-most vision that set my mind back to zero, like a child, as I struggled to understand how to interact in this world again – this world of imaginary objects and entities. For the rest of my life I have watched as the most fleeting and buried intentions - the ones we don't even think we have – manifest in external situations within our health or circumstances or in others. Undigested impulse and well-suppressed emotion snake out to wreak havoc externally. They create material situations and tangible real-world repercussions. I see that one of the greatest jobs I'm given in this life is to wrestle these very human energies into unified, directed control of a heart- and mind-empowered will.

This is why in our physical and emotional health, healing modalities from the spiritual or energetic level - the level of intentions taking form - are often the most effective approach. Intervention at this higher level, if grace allows it, stirs change through all the layers of our being at once and allows us to integrate the power from our health challenge rather than trying to cut it out or suppress it.

Comprehension did not return to the body on the hospital bed at the same time my awareness did. Awe, bewilderment, and a sense of being part of the fabric of the drama rather than a separate actor remained when I came to see the nurse checking my vitals, the sleepy husband sitting, waiting, both of them obviously actors in the piece we'd agreed to play together in some long-forgotten union of purpose. I felt like an ant who had transformed in a flash to a human and then right back to ant, left in shock trying to understand what had just happened. I was bewildered, and unable to bring what I had just learned back through the eye of the needle with me. From the perspective of the One it was all simple and self-evident. But when trying to swim through daily life after finding out it's as good as imaginary – well, that's confusing.

We - the nurse and the husband and I - were like aspen trees, appearing separate but all secretly one gnarly ancient organism, roots tangled in self-relation. Nonduality pervaded – a sense of being them, of them being me, of all three of us and even the fixtures and the air in the hospital room itself playing temporary roles together by taking form here and now.

A burning duality reared back – separation from other. Surely they were already in on this! Does everyone in the world already know? How could I ever have forgotten? The truth of connection was the soup we were swimming in, self-evident as the air we breathe. It was everywhere, penetrating our bodies, and the personas we shared with each other were like costumes in a drama. And I (little I, the little separate human) felt truly dumbfounded to have forgotten what is everywhere and obvious and felt like a fool: for everyone else must surely already know that the world we're pretending to act in together is not at all what it seems!

TENACIOUS SPROUT

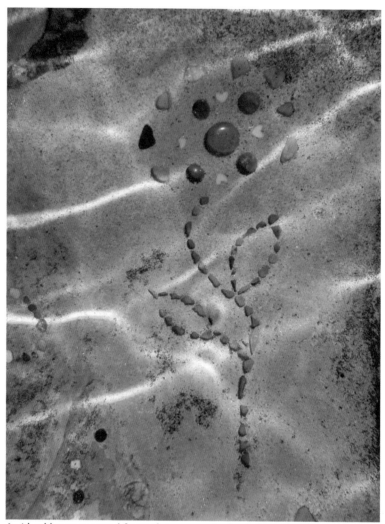

As I had been assured from the moment of returning into this life, my body was not destroyed. At an inner insistence I refused the offered surgeries to stabilize the pieces of the pelvis. The expected internal bleeding and organ damage never came to pass. Because I was recovering unexpectedly well, I was released early from the hospital, sent home to a lot of flowers and health equipment including my very own fashionable living room hospital bed, trapeze and wheelchair. This equipment was all released early as well. Medical professionals who worked with my injuries repeatedly expressed surprise at my survival and rapid recovery. I shuffled and dragged along for awhile, but over time and with the help of skilled craniosacral therapists my movement became smoother. I recovered extremely well from the initial injuries despite years of chronic pain.

Before the accident, I had been a rational computer programmer, distantly and loosely Protestant from a childhood of fairly open-minded church Sundays. I had always sensed a sacred inner relationship with something higher, but put very little stock in it being anything like the Bible taught. I mainly didn't think about it, young as I was. Coming from a blue-collar Montana community, married young, and recently graduated from college, I was open to some possibilities of paranormal phenomena but had strong skeptical and sarcastic streaks and an abstract and reductionist mind.

Despite my average American background, the pain-fueled laser focus on the breath for hours over days had thrust me completely unprepared into a deep state that was the goal of yogis and seekers worldwide throughout the ages, a state of perception some cultures have called Samadhi.

What followed were many years of vivid, ongoing transcendent experiences that struck whenever they pleased, leaving me rushing to get to a place of solitude before being knocked to my knees in grateful tears. Revelatory visions and psychophysical sensations brought insight, ecstasy, direction and healing – sometimes dramatic healing. I wanted nothing but to be alone and drunk with it. I spent many, many hours alone running ridges, or lying about on a mountainside, soaking up the motherly grounding of the earth as the intense currents of the vital forces coursed through me. Sometimes I was moved into spontaneous postures or movements (similar to yoga asanas or kriyas) without having an understanding of what they were to the ancients, but they channeled the exquisite lightning through my spine in increasingly useful ways. Several health practitioners who saw me during these years remarked on something strange about an unusual and unreadable neuro-electrical system (when their testing equipment and methods didn't work as usual), and I stopped wearing a watch after burning through battery after battery. All of these sensations and phenomena I now know can be common for people who are undergoing an experience called kundalini awakening. You might also just call it waking up.

From the week of the accident on, I was equipped with a few new unwavering aspects to my perspective. Most of them are common to many people who have had similar experiences:

> an unraveling belief in any existing paradigm of thought
> an unrelenting obligation to notice everything within my subconscious space
>
> an unquenchable desire to serve the light, to share what I had come to understand within (and the maddening combination of having no way of showing or telling it and the firm conviction that it couldn't be conveyed to most people most of the time anyway)
>
> a sense of peace and trust that the hurdles and difficulties in my life were deliberately and wisely self-chosen for a highly-desired purpose. It is hard to express what a gift this awareness was. So much of our suffering comes from wondering 'Why?' and 'What if?'. Without these poisons – recrimination and remorse - I was free to cleanly endure my battle wounds and transform them
>
> a sense of higher presence with me that has never left
> a buoyant sense of wellbeing deep within despite physical and emotional turmoil on the surface
>
> a sense of detachment from the interactions and personal relationships in my life, a sense of pretending to be this person (this came and went for a few years)
>
> a sense of having already accomplished and learned whatever the 'goal' was in life, while at the very same time being very painfully aware that I had no concept of any of the details that bridge the two ways of knowing. I was unable to manifest even a small part of that kernel of wisdom within, and was an empty and shallow novice in so many things that mattered to living the kind of life I respected. I felt the strangest combination of all-knowing and knowing nothing whatsoever, of having intimate proximity to the ultimate

source of power and at the same time having great difficulty getting my hands on top of my head to wash my own hair. The fast food-loving computer programmer from a lumber town had no idea how to work with the clear-eyed, burning-hearted, child-minded devotee that had taken charge within, and the work of rebuilding a broken body and life gave them both something to do while they sorted themselves out.

The Vedics called the sacrum the sacred bone, seat of the soul, where the coiled snake of Kundalini Shakti resides. This energetic force unleashed in my spine when the pelvis was broken open, a force that burns like electricity through my skin and senses and spirit and every decision I make. It has unfolded and intensified in my life ever since, leading inexorably to growth. My antennae – nervous system - is changed forever. My job here is to burn through emotional and energetic burdens, to transform whatever comes up, and there's no turning away from it. (Plenty of stumbling, but no turning away!) Wherever this leads, I'm married to the path.

Slowly, I left much allopathic medicine behind. I'm grateful it's there when heroic measures are needed like severe pain control and emergency surgery. But the wide application of western invasive and reductionist medical tools to chronic, subtle, lifestyle and energetic challenges is a tragedy of awesome scale. So many other cultures offer a gentler way through the health conditions we turn into crises. For moving through much of daily life - and through most of our emergencies – I've found most effective changes with holistic and energetic means. And time after time these intelligent remedies have opened worlds that feel no less than miraculous. Recognizing the state of my health as a mirror for inner work has been an important part of my journey.

After a few years I endured an inevitable dark night of the soul, common to many people going through spiritual upheaval: depression, swooning and careening id and ego, both ecstatic and depressive isolation, gnostic revelations, physical agony and dysfunction. Chronic arthritis and fibromyalgia-like pain left me worried about how my children would grow up with a mama cranky as I was to be touched. Psychologically I felt like I was climbing and sliding down fractals, my perspective coming from a nearby but dramatically different scale and scope than it was supposed to be. My emotions were wickedly labile, and for years there was a vivid sense of existing on multiple planes at once, as if some part of me was in an intensive apprenticeship with the language of symbols, of alchemy, of the esoteric and sublime, when at the same time my actual daily life involved running around after little ones all day. To understand what was happening to me and how it had unfolded for others, I found my way to the books of other cultures and subcultures in traditions that recognized the body's intrinsic relationship with spirit: Kundalini, Tantra, Jungian symbolism, shamanic literature. There seemed to be a core of radiance getting stronger within me every day, even while I was trapped in the lumbering, stiff prison my body had become. I could see these other worlds were available to step into. This hitting bottom was an essential part of the path, and I needed the help of homeopathy, plant medicine, nutrition, movement and energetic self-healing – and conscious surrender – to climb out of it. With the grace of the stars, I was given the opportunity to essentially step onto the other potential, parallel threads of life that had continued with or without me. One afternoon I felt a powerful energetic fountain rise with me, the masculine and feminine meeting in the middle, and experienced an inner sense of solar graduation: it was now time to begin turning outward again. Replacing those years of confusion and disruption grew a new sense of stability, power and insight.

Large chunks of useful information began to appear out of the ether in response to grass waves rippling in the wind, or the shape of a cloud, or a distant door slam... Sometimes when I was near or put my hands on people, I would sense their emotions and pains and heartaches and remedies. Medicinal plants seemed to be singing to me from the trailside, calling to be of use, and I discovered a determined passion for earth medicine and the joy of plant communication. As is common to most people experiencing a process of spiritual awakening, my sexuality underwent a radical shift. Orgasms deepened, moved to swallow my whole body and wash through air that surrounded me, and became effective gifts for in flowing stuck patterns of consciousness through the body. Eventually they even became a powerful form of connection for drawing built-up energy and directing it the conscious influence of changes we wish: healing, crafting creative experiences, clearing emotional blocks.

(Like the great twilight - dying - all of life's in-betweens offer a powerful edge where the veil is thinner. Between sleep and wake, during life transition, in dreams, between body-bound human and orgasmic ecstasy, in the euphoria of chemical change during exercise, during unsettling great emotion or physical sensation when your ground is unsteady... all are powerful times to deepen your practice and your connection to the Source.)

Almost ten years ago I began noticing the strong influence of communication with our unborn children, and dropped hormonal and barrier forms of contraception. Actively projecting a "No" in the years we didn't want a pregnancy, we sensed their desire to join us as if a cosmic window of fertility had opened, and when we were ready emotionally, invited them in. I remember one night silently extending an invitation to my son to join us, as he had been hovering and waiting. Just days later two chatty voices let me overhear "She's pregnant, you know." The other said, "Yes, with a strapping boy." He himself told me he would be born a little early and it should be at home. Without ever taking a pregnancy test or having missed a day of my cycle, we were announcing our son's upcoming birth to friends and family. And he is in fact strapping, was born a bit early, channels energy beautifully with his hands, and has a knack for communicating with wild medicinal plants. Two talented midwives helped us welcome both my daughter and son in homebirths because before and throughout pregnancy the babies – and my own inner guide - impressed to me how important it was for them and for my health as well. (With a pelvis and sacrum that had been shattered, it wasn't easy. But the natural births left them with radiant health and a gentle energetic entry, and left me with a far healthier pelvis and hips.) Last year we were shocked to witness my daughter at the age of seven doggedly stride off-path in the Sonoran desert, strike spontaneous yoga poses facing the red setting sun, and break down at the moment of sunset in a transcendent experience that left her crying in wonder for hours, staring at her hands as she cried "I'm so happy to be a little girl!", and swearing off "birthday parties and ice cream and swimming, as long as I could stay right here forever being part of the rocks and plants". She has found her inner compass.

These stories are a small beacon of something larger. Because our world is so rapidly changing, more and more people around the world are experiencing a catalyzing of this vital force. It takes hold and leads a person into their next evolution. Along the way – piece by painstaking piece – it remodels the neuroendocrine system, the libido, the reproductive organs, the emotions, the senses, the intellect and flesh itself. A healthy kundalini force opens our senses to a new dimension of Knowing and Being and Doing. It may tear us open like lightning as it rises, or it may wash in on gently manageable waves. But this is the season: it's unfolding in more and more people. Legions are awakening to reclaim a birthright.

GLEANINGS

Although I was changed forever in the single instant of the accident, it took a long time to even begin manifesting what I'd learned in the daily actions of life, and I will never fully accomplish it because every day I wake up and, what do you know?, I'm still a highly flawed human. How can we ever bridge the Earthly and Unity ways of knowing? What rules do you play by when you discover your world is imaginary? I stumbled around for years before coming up with some useful guidelines that tried to filter some of the wisdom back into this life where it all looks upside down. Here are some hard-learned lessons. Some I wish I could offer that 22-year-old as she first began recreating her life after the accident, and some she taught me. Maybe they'll be familiar to you from a place within.

LEARN HOW TO DIRECT YOUR WILL AND ENERGY CONSCIOUSLY

The experience of the web of consciousness brought tremendous weight to bear in my own efforts to tame and become aware of the energies I am putting out there. They slip right out and shape consciousness into reality, and if you are fooling yourself about the subtle emotions you're allowing yourself to have, they are still causing ripples in your life. Our self-honest intentions matter more than we know. The way I like to deal with slippery intentions is not to ignore or suppress them, but to be aware, to notice, to fully experience and listen and digest, then to align and transform the energies through genuine personal emotional alchemy, raising the issue up into the light and beaming the emotions out that would instead be healthiest, integrating the experience into myself. I have found that if you can resolve the situation within you, it usually resolves outside of you as well.

BECAUSE EVERYTHING IS CONSCIOUSNESS, ANYTHING IS POSSIBLE

There isn't anything you can imagine that can't be, because it's all a play of consciousness. Us included. The further I go along this route, the more strange things I hear and see. Nothing is impossible.

AS LONG AS LIFE ITSELF GOES ON, YOU DO TOO

As long as life itself does, in any form, in any world, in any plane of existence, you go on too. Only the frame for the witness shifts. We go on. We exist as life itself, as divinity itself, and we ARE the face of God in this world, every single messed up one of us, every single rock and tree. We Are God. We Are Divine. At the same time, we're inherently limited and blemished as humans. Just do the best you can.

AS A PART OF DIVINE CONSCIOUSNESS, YOU ARE DIVINE

"When my mind was cleansed of impurities,
like a mirror of its dust and dirt,
I recognized the Self in me:
When I saw Him dwelling in me,
I realized that He was the Everything
and I was nothing.
I saw and found I am in everything
I saw God effulgent in everything.
After hearing and pausing see Siva
The House is His alone; Who am I, Lalla." Lallashwari

We each have within us the same light that shined within Krishna and Jesus and the Buddha and everyone who's ever carried the torch. We are each Divinity's opportunity to experience and create a unique face of life, to allow it to shine right through our inevitable, insufferable flaws. And when that particular life form is done, we recycle back into the ocean – a wave that dances and melts back in, to re-form and experience anew.

FEAR NOTHING – LEAST OF ALL DEATH

"The heart that breaks open can contain the whole universe." Joanna Macy

It's all chosen – by you - through love. There is always a healing path right through the middle of it. The worst you can imagine – the very worst – may even be rejoiced on the other side, and none of it ever goes unnoticed. You have infinite support available to you, whole worlds cheering for you to weather it well and grow with love so you can come home. BE BOLD.

JOY IN INCARNATION
"We have been raised to fear the yes within ourselves, our deepest cravings." Audre Lorde
"And your very flesh shall be a great poem." Walt Whitman

Your higher self incarnated because as a sensate, embodied being you can have experiences your spirit alone cannot. Don't be afraid of desire. Don't be afraid of passion, of adventure, of a little sin, of failure, of living in your own unique way. Don't be afraid of anything. Life truly is a big play – have fun with it, don't take it so seriously. Life in all its glory goes on, no matter how messy it looks from here and now.

TACKLE IT NOW
"The problem is not to find the answer, it's to face the answer." Terence McKenna

You know that part of yourself you're putting off thinking about? Maybe it's a relationship or habit. The part you know down deep isn't quite lined up with the rest of you? Tackle it now. The pattern's not going to go away without your attention, and eventually (maybe after a few more lives) you will resolve it. Wouldn't it be more pleasant to just do it now and move on along the spiral?

SELF-HEALING IS YOUR BIRTHRIGHT: THE KEY IS PAYING ATTENTION
"The body has a wisdom of its own. However, slowly and circuitously that wisdom manifests, once it is experienced it is a foundation, a basis of knowing that gives confidence to the ego. To reach its wisdom requires absolute concentration: dropping the mind into the body, breathing into whatever is ready to be released, and allowing the process of expression until the negative dammed up energy is out, making room for the positive energy, genuine Light, to flood in."
Marion Woodman

We each have the power to heal. With listening, intention and through some gift: our hands, music, presence, words, plants, nourishment, nurturing... We each have the power to immerse ourselves in direct communication with nature, receiving revelation and insight. We each have the power to use sexual energy as a sacred transformational force. We each have the power to interact with the subtle energies that make up our bodies and world. We have the gift of influencing our fertility and contraception through communication with our unborn children. KNOWING you have the power makes the difference. And practice, because that will bring it into manifestation. Examine your shadow fearlessly, bringing your unconscious energies into new relationship and alignment with the whole. When we can lovingly recognize our dark and light, and respect the information brought to us by our dark, our flaws, our challenges, our pain, we can begin to channel the energies more effectively and responsibly and put their power to work for us.

THE MACROCOSM IS THE MICROCOSM

As within, so without. Once you decide to recognize the mirror, you will see how to change its reflection. At this time of increased social, political and environmental change it is even more important to tend to the fires within. We can make the greatest changes in the world by starting with ourselves. Whenever I have an outward situation catch my attention, like a sprained ankle, or strained relationship, it means it is time to settle and look inward for the cause. There is always an energetic root, and it's an effective place to leverage change.

May your body be blessed.

May you realize that your body is a
faithful and beautiful friend of your soul.

May you recognize that
your senses are sacred thresholds.

May you realize that holiness is
mindful gazing, mindful feeling, mindful listening,
and mindful touching.

May your senses always enable you
to celebrate the universe and the mystery and possibilities
in your presence here.

May Eros bless you.
May your senses gather you and bring you Home.

THE BODY ALWAYS WINS - YOUR BODY IS THE TEMPLE

"Only by discovering and loving the goddess lost within our rejected body can we hear our own authentic voice. This is your body, your greatest gift, pregnant with wisdom you do not hear, grief you thought was forgotten, and joy you have never known." Marion Woodman

"There are many kinds of power, used and unused, acknowledged or otherwise. The erotic is a resource within each of us that lies in a deeply female and spiritual plane, firmly rooted in the power of our unexpressed or unrecognized feeling. In order to perpetuate itself, every oppression must corrupt or distort those various sources of power within the culture of the oppressed that can provide energy for change. For women, this has meant a suppression of the erotic as a considered source of power and information within our lives.
This is one reason why the erotic is so feared, and so often relegated to the bedroom alone, when it is recognized at all. For once we begin to feel deeply all the aspects of our lives, we begin to demand from ourselves and from our life-pursuits that they feel in accordance with that joy which we know ourselves to be capable of. Our erotic knowledge empowers us, becomes a lens through which we scrutinize all aspects of our existence, forcing us to evaluate those aspects honestly in terms of their relative meaning within our lives. And this is a grave responsibility, projected from within each of us, not to settle for the convenient, the shoddy, the conventionally expected, nor the merely safe." Audre Lorde

Our bodies signal the way through. Sometimes it's through a sense of uneasiness in the gut, a sense of 'Yes' in the heart, sometimes a tightness in the throat from holding back one's own truth. Once we begin decoding it, our bodies hold infinite information. It is our radar, our antennae, for moment to moment guidance through life. And we can try to overrule it at our peril.

It's so human to get caught up in life and refuse to listen to our emotions, and their physical symptoms, because we're needed in many other directions. We discount the signals our body is giving because – down deep – we know what it is going to ask us to do and are not ready to face it. So ultimately, the body takes us down with a chronic pain syndrome or disease until we listen and make the changes demanded by the higher spirit working through the body. We can offer self-care early, when it will involve pleasure. Or we can wait to make changes until we're forced to, when it will involve pain. But ultimately, the body always wins because it is the domain of the subconscious. This is a complicated intersection here with disability and neurodiversity, with trauma and systemic oppression. But within our individual journeys, our nervous system and fascia are the connection to other realms. Nourish and cleanse the body with food and movement every day, listen to its wisdom, and feel free to negotiate for clearer communication.

PRACTICE TURNING YOUR THOUGHTS HIGHER
To my great surprise at some point during the near-death experience, the smallness of my last thoughts on earth stood out as one of the few things that would be a shame about my death - "Oh, this is going to be a big one. I'm costing us money again." The death itself wouldn't have been much of a loss to the fabric of life itself, but those poor, tiny last thoughts were a loss. It seems like we need to hold the highest state we can – ideally through every moment of life, but at least as we pass through the needle. So I try to practice both embodying the senses, and bringing my emotions to the most beautiful interpretation of what is – boundless love, a keening gratitude, joy and peace, courage. Surround yourself with books, music and other art that uplifts you, that brings you to a better self, and practice getting there in an instant. Just in case the mountainside comes at you fast.

WE ARE NEVER OUTSIDE THE LIGHT
Blessed be those who are cracked, for the cracks are where the light shines through.

"This being human is a guest house.
Every morning a new arrival.
A joy, a depression, a meanness,
some momentary awareness comes
as an unexpected visitor.
Welcome and entertain them all!
Even if they are a crowd of sorrows,
who violently sweep your house
empty of its furniture,
still, treat each guest honorably.
He may be clearing you out

for some new delight.
The dark thought, the shame, the malice.
meet them at the door laughing and invite them in.
Be grateful for whatever comes.
because each has been sent
as a guide from beyond." Rumi

The veil just makes us think we have dark within us. We may turn away, hide our faces. But the source of all keeps shining on us anyway, waiting for us to look up and notice. Every day I try to remind all the parts of me to let the light stream through despite unending flaws, despite every day still weaving myself through the human impulses that distract from the stronger desire to be in Oneness. If you squint just right, ugly turns beautiful.

When I think of that primal desire at the root of all others, I picture all of us humans like salmon leaping upstream, each in our own way, choosing our own path, our own thrust (maybe even secretly tsk-tsk-ing a neighbor salmon's trajectory). We're all after the same thing whether we know it or not. From the sublime artist to the drunk to the emotional manipulator, we are all seeking reunion. Our decisions make their own logic within the context of where we are and what's in our way to get back home, and it's easy to hurt each other by misreading this pure universal desire.

BAD THINGS AREN'T ALWAYS BAD
"The heart that breaks open can contain the whole universe." Joanna Macy

I believe when we are struck with challenges and suffering and we weather them with the most open heart and clear eyes we can – without blame or recrimination, without grasping, accepting responsibility for all our own circumstances (while working to define the boundaries and structures that need to change) – we are each claiming a small win for the whole of life. We freely chose our family, our flaws, our recurring fights - as impossible as it can be to imagine from here.

May this fortify us as we witness the crushing systemic traumas in our societies, and weave stronger fabric and structure by facing what is, and what's within our power to change.

THE MAP IS NOT THE TERRITORY

"Truth has no path. Truth is living, and therefore, changing. It has no resting place, no form, no organized institution, no philosophy... This evening I see something totally new and that newness is experienced by the mind, but tomorrow that experience becomes mechanical if I try to repeat the sensation, the pleasure of it. The description is never real. What is real is seeing the truth instantaneously, because truth has no tomorrow." Bruce Lee

"The words of my book nothing, the drift of it everything.... Do I contradict myself? Very well, then I contradict myself, I am large, I contain multitudes." Walt Whitman

For the first ten years after the accident I had rare words for any of this and it remained a burning, insanity-producing secret inside of me that I had no way to unlock. It was physically difficult to open my mouth to discuss it! When I first was experiencing these states, not only did my lips not want to move (it can't be put into words), but I couldn't even make the conceptual part of my brain move (it can't be put into concepts). All of me resisted, wanting nothing to disturb the pervading peace. And as soon as a word started in my mind space, even a nice word like 'Truth' or 'Love', it diminished the Whole. It implied there was something (truth) and so carved part away from the whole, inherently implying that there is also not something (untruth). It is partially for this same reason that for years afterward I had difficulty using the word 'I' without inwardly grimacing at the lie of it all. There is no 'I'. The sense of I can be shifted to be limitless - it's only a sense of boundary and perspective. So right here, in this very sentence, I'm lying despite my best efforts. Do you see the problem here? How simple questions like "How are you?" can become a trap if you're trying to be painstakingly truthful? Not one of those words can be parsed unambiguously. There was no longer a perspective from which to solidly answer innocent questions.

One. Everything we ever need to know comes straight from that one inescapable thing. Call it the Tao, the unity, collective consciousness, or God. Labels only confuse the situation. The map is not the territory.

If anything I say doesn't resonate with you, toss it out. YOU are the only one who can decide truth for yourself. Take nothing at face value, no matter the authority. They may be speaking truth at their level, but only you can decide if it's a paradigm that's useful to you. We are all using the metaphors and perspectives and senses and cultural overlays available to us, and there are hundreds of beautiful books describing similar experiences in modern cultural concepts and terms. Once we break the code of reading metaphorically, most of the world's sacred books can partially be read as deeply informative symbolism for this same living process as it moves through the various layers and energies of a human being's life and body.

God is too big to fit inside one religion. Refuse to cling to any definition of what "God" is! It's certainly not an embodied being or a masculine entity. (The systemic imbalance of a single-gender God is absurd on the face of it.) Even the word "God" felt like sacrilege to me for years, like condensing the ultimate force into a shoebox with sides: there were so many cultural projections onto the concept of "God" of personification, and my experience was not of God as a separate paternal force. Instead I interpret this potent word as the underlying, glorious, intelligent, sublimely loving force that simply IS, leaping again and again into existence through all of us. By this definition, and by my experience, there is nothing that is not God.

Every religion has a branch devoted to the mystical perspective – the Christians have the Gnostics, the Jews the Kabbalists, Muslims the Sufi, Hindi the Jain. I had to reach out to the writings of the mystics and the sacred texts of other cultures, ones who have not separated the body away from the spirit, to understand the process that was beginning to open up in my body electric. I recognize a little inherent kinship with some of the currents of Vajrayana Buddhism (Tantra): the path of using everything in life for fuel for burning off the veil - all that is, pleasure and pain, including the dark within us, those things we like to stuff into the shadow. Obsessive reading of archetypal Jungian psychology was crucial in building the dictionary of my own inner messages. But these are labels. Volumes of reading can offer comfort in gaining cultural reference for similar experiences. Reading and sharing help us know we're not alone in our human journey. But ultimately, we must bow only to the guru within.

THE GURU IS WITHIN YOU
"I believe a leaf of grass is no less than the journey-work of the stars."
Walt Whitman

"The sun shines not on us but in us. The rivers flow not past, but through us. Thrilling, tingling, vibrating every fiber and cell of the substance of our bodies, making them glide and sing. The trees wave and the flowers bloom in our bodies as well as our souls, and every bird song, wind song, and tremendous storm song of the rocks in the heart of the mountains is our song, our very own, and sings our love." John Muir

Everything you ever want to know can open up with enough intense focus. A breeze moving a leaf, birdsong at just the right moment, the voice of running water, that soft sense of warmth in your heart.... it is your birthright to learn how to hear the answers springing from the fabric of life around you.
Pay attention.

Throw out your books and allow the living rhythms to engulf you.

Printed in Great Britain
by Amazon

50016774R00022